P E N N S Y L V A N I A

Marjorie Ackermann

William Weidman

PENNSYLVANIA

Photography by H. MARK WEIDMAN

Essay by Marjorie Ackermann

GRAPHIC ARTS CENTER PUBLISHING™

International Standard Book Number 1-55868-159-0
Library of Congress Catalog Number 93-73315
Photographs © MCMXCIV by H. Mark Weidman
H. Mark Weidman Photography • 215/646-1745
Text and captions © MCMXCIV by Graphic Arts Center Publishing®
P.O. Box 10306 • Portland, Oregon 97210 • 503/226-2402
President • Charles M. Hopkins
Editor-in-Chief • Douglas A. Pfeiffer
Managing Editor • Jean Andrews
Production Manager • Richard L. Owsiany
Designer • Robert Reynolds
Cartographer • Ortelius Design
Typographer • Harrison Typesetting, Inc.
Book Manufacturing • Lincoln & Allen Company
Printed in the United States of America
Second Printing

Every August, the finest young ball teams compete in the Little League World Series in Williamsport. Little League began here in 1939 with thirty players, and has grown to 2.7 million worldwide. ◀◀ The drama of small-town life unfolds at the Waterford bandstand, a gathering spot for weddings, square dances, Memorial Day speeches, and summer concerts. ◀

To our families,
and especially to our son Christopher Neal

H. Mark Weidman and Marjorie Ackermann

PENNSYLVANIA

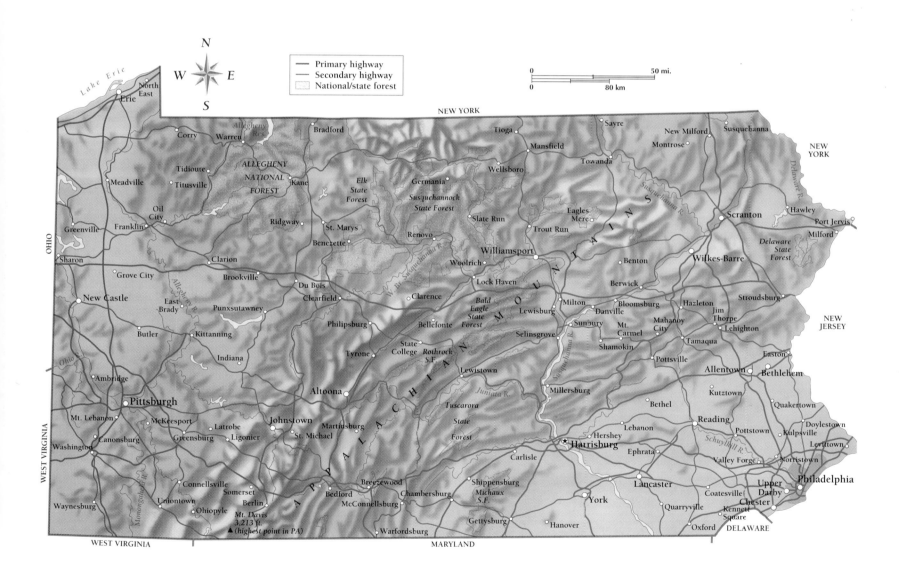

Preface

by H. Mark Weidman

THE MAGIC OF THIS PROJECT was the people I met. What a joy it is to work with people who love what they do. For them, work is not a chore. I will never forget the way logger Dave Feidler skillfully felled a cherry tree, so it would not damage other trees on its way to the forest floor. Nor will I forget the way Winston Strahan, his arms tight with muscle, polished every tabletop at Pennsylvania House Furniture as if it were going into *his* living room.

Author and Penn State professor Joe Humphreys caught four trout for my camera on a cool May morning when no one else even had a bite. Joe worried that I did not have waders to protect me from the cold, clear waters of the Yellow Breeches Creek, but I shrugged off his concern and waded in chest deep. After an hour of shooting, I suddenly understood what fifty years of fishing had taught Joe. When I climbed from the stream, my legs were so numb I could not walk for ten full minutes!

I relied on a different kind of expert to photograph the unique Presque Isle peninsula near Erie. Pilot Jim Lee designs, builds, and sells an experimental aircraft that looks like a supercharged ultralight. A propellor is mounted behind the overhead wings. Two seats, which look like lawn chairs, are bolted to an aluminum frame at the front of the craft. Wearing a crash helmet and goggles, Jim flew us at sunset through ten-knot winds. Only a seat belt was between me and Lake Erie below, but our hawk's perspective was fantastic for photography. After we landed, I asked Jim about the bomblike device, labeled "Second Chance," mounted over the wings. It was a rocket-propelled parachute to be used as a last resort in an emergency. He had never tried it.

Bouncing along in rowing coach Bruce Lalonde's skiff, I gained great appreciation for the strength and grace inherent in sculling and began to understand what motivates the women of the Philadelphia Girls Rowing Club. Three times a week they ply the waters of the Schuylkill River, often finishing before sunrise and in time for work or school.

Mountain laurel, Pennsylvania's state flower, blooms in Cowans Gap State Park and throughout "Penn's Woods" each June. ◄

In Pittsburgh, I was privileged to photograph Dr. Thomas Starzl and Fred Rogers. Dr. Starzl, who has dedicated a lifetime to solving the puzzle of organ transplantation, has a humble, gracious style that led the portrait session far beyond the scheduled time frame. He told me that while growing up in LeMars, Iowa, he read every book at the local Carnegie Library, part of Pittsburgh industrialist Andrew Carnegie's legacy. Of all the places he has lived, Pittsburgh is his favorite. Fred Rogers' calling in life is to create a better world for our children, our future. Because of camera noise, still photographers are generally not welcome in television studios, but "Mister Rogers' Neighborhood" was more than accommodating.

Many Pennsylvanians trusted me, for which I am grateful. After a blizzard, Tom Polonia of Wellsboro—whom I had never met before—lent me his snowmobile, which enabled me to travel to the Grand Canyon of Pennsylvania. Caretaker Bill Lloyd of Fallingwater stayed late one winter night so I could make a dusk photo of the Frank Lloyd Wright house in fresh snow. He was excited to help create a different kind of image of the famous house. And the congregation at Philadelphia's Mother Bethel Church trusted me to document them during some of their most private moments—while in prayer.

Pennsylvania is known for its beautiful landscape and abundant wildlife. I wonder where we would be without the dedicated people in our parks and preserves—like Shelby Rudolph, who nurses injured raptors at Hawk Mountain Sanctuary, or naturalist Patrick Adams, who showed me his favorite wildflower spots in Raccoon Creek State Park. Their enthusiasm was infectious. My appreciation for the natural world grew stronger with each journey into Pennsylvania's woods.

We Pennsylvanians live in a state rich in natural beauty and filled with wonderful people. I hope I have portrayed both the land and the people with the respect they deserve.

Completed in 1756, the Pennsylvania State House, now known as Independence Hall, is the place where Congress adopted the Declaration of Independence and drafted the U.S. Constitution. ◄ An American linden tree stands guard at Valley Forge, site of the Continental Army's grueling winter encampment of 1777-78. The Revolutionary War post became Pennsylvania's first state park in 1893 and a national park in 1976. ▲

Hearts Content Scenic Area encompasses a 121-acre remnant of virgin woodlands. This national natural landmark—popular for hiking and cross-country skiing—is in Allegheny National Forest. ▲ Hopewell Furnace relied on "horsepower" to transport the supplies necessary for its ironmaking operation. This barn sheltered less than half the horses needed. ▶

Each fall, bird-watchers from around the world scour the skies above Hawk Mountain Sanctuary for thousands of raptors, such as red-tailed hawks, which migrate along the Kittatinny Ridge. ◄ When Pennsylvania purchased the land for Moraine State Park, it was scarred by coal mines, gas and oil wells, and acid-mine drainage. The state reclaimed the land and constructed a lake pure enough for fishing and swimming. ▲

Pittsburgh's close-knit neighborhoods, like Bloomfield, are home to almost one hundred ethnic groups. The small-town feeling is a key to Pittsburgh's reputation as one of the safest, most livable cities. ▲ A farm stand entices shoppers in North East, a lakeside community near Erie that is known as the largest grape-growing region east of the Mississippi. ▶

My Pennsylvania Backyard

by Marjorie Ackermann

AS A GIRL, I LOVED TRAVELING on the Pennsylvania Turnpike. From my home west of Philadelphia, the turnpike interchange was just a short drive away, but taking the turnpike was no ordinary event. We never used it for trips to school or the supermarket or to visit my grandparents in Northeast Philly. No, passing through the toll booth at Norristown meant only one thing in my childhood: my parents, my two sisters, and I were going on a bona fide journey.

The eastbound lanes hurtled us to the flatlands of New Jersey and the maddening traffic ensnarling New York City. The northeastern extension sped us to the Poconos, where my sisters and I went to summer camp near Dingmans Falls. Like generations of vacationers before us, we hiked on forest trails cushioned with pine needles, canoed across a cool, blue lake, and splashed in waterfalls that left our hair baby soft.

The westbound lanes led to Lancaster County and the Amish, but beyond that they seemed to stretch endlessly—to Pittsburgh and the Midwest, through the Great Plains, across the mighty Rockies, until finally I imagined that the seamless interstates met their match in the vast Pacific. When we headed west on the turnpike, I felt the whole country unfolding before me. Anything was possible.

Today, I still live near Philadelphia and feel the same tug of adventure when I point my car toward Harrisburg. But on this trip, my route is a circular one around a state I have called home for almost forty years. I plan to head west across Pennsylvania's southern tier to Pittsburgh, then return east along the state's northern tier, before swinging back south to Philadelphia. With about forty-six thousand square miles to explore, I could spend a lifetime crisscrossing the state's sixty-seven counties. Since most of my travels have taken me out of Pennsylvania, this time I want to sample what lies in my own backyard. My journey, like the journeys of my youth, begins by heading west on the turnpike.

Shawnees Dan Moluntha Wright
and Ken Shooting Star wear
their traditional dress at
High Knob Overlook in
the Endless Mountains. ◄

I leave home on a cloudy September morning and find traffic heavy, as usual, approaching the turnpike's busiest interchange, Valley Forge. Offices, hotels, shopping malls, and residences border the open fields of the national park where General Washington's troops endured the winter of 1777-78. Confined to cramped log huts with little to eat and less to wear, the Continental army was ravaged by typhus, typhoid fever, dysentery, and pneumonia. No battle was ever fought at Valley Forge, but the ordeal proved a moral victory for Washington's men. The Continentals emerged from the six-month encampment a stronger, more cohesive fighting force.

In spring, when the dogwoods bloom and cyclists and joggers crowd the park's trails, Valley Forge seems more a piece of heaven than hell. But in winter, when snow covers the reconstructed huts and an icy wind blows through the chinking, you can almost see the ragged soldiers huddled around each stone fireplace.

Once I pass Valley Forge, the rolling hills of Chester County surround me. This is horse country, where miles of post-and-rail fences enclose picture-perfect fields. Tradition and privilege are rooted in this verdant land of fox hunts and country estates. At the Devon Horse Show each May, more than a hundred thousand spectators watch their favorites compete in the country's oldest outdoor equestrian show. One of the most popular—and festive—events is the Carriage Pleasure Drive. Men dressed in top hats and tails and women bedecked in hats with veils and feathers drive their carriages through the affluent Main Line neighborhoods near the fairgrounds. Watching the shiny black coaches and meticulously groomed horses trot by is like stepping into a Jane Austen novel.

As I near the Reading exit, billboards tout the "Outlet Capital of the World." A century ago, hosiery mills flourished in Reading, but as the textile industry moved south or overseas, the huge knitting machines

Lancaster County's fertile farmland

grew quiet. In the 1960s, a few clothing manufacturers in the mills started selling their imperfects and over-runs to employees. The demand for these bargains soon grew, and the old mills became home to the new and now booming outlet industry.

The potent smell of manure wafts into my car, and I know I have arrived in Lancaster County. From the air, the county looks like a carefully planned mosaic where contoured fields of corn, tobacco, and hay surround sturdy farmhouses and barns. In recent years housing developments and industrial parks have sprouted, but the farms of the Amish and closely related Mennonites still dominate the landscape. The Plain People till these rich Piedmont soils, using the time-honored methods of their ancestors, to make this the most productive non-irrigated county in the nation.

I leave the turnpike in the heart of Pennsylvania Dutch Country and proceed south on Route 222 to Ephrata. I pass acres of golden, withered cornstalks and spot an Amish buggy crossing an overpass. Cultivating the land and keeping apart from outside influences underlie the Amish world. Shunned for their religious beliefs in their native Switzerland, the Amish migrated to Pennsylvania in the early 1700s. The strictest sect, the Old Order Amish, eschew modern conveniences such as cars, electricity, and telephones. Other Amish sects are less strict, permitting the use of dark-colored cars, for instance. While the romanticized image of the Amish focuses on their plain, dark clothing and horse-drawn buggies, some Amish also drink sodas, play softball, and build wooden swing sets.

With up to five million tourists visiting Lancaster County each year, the Amish are not strangers to the ways of the "English," as they call outsiders. Amish craftsmanship is prized, and they sell their goods far beyond their insular community. Amish men built the shed in my backyard, and Amish women stitched my Trip-Around-the-World quilt.

The Amish and Mennonites were not the only sects to escape religious persecution by settling in Lancaster County. In Ephrata, German mystic Conrad Beissel and his followers founded a cloister in 1732 where the celibate brothers and sisters lived an austere, calibrated life. The community also admitted married members, but they lived a less circumscribed life on nearby farms.

Some of the cloister's stark, medieval-style buildings still stand, and I arrive at this historic site searching for clues to the meaning of William Penn's Holy Experiment. Penn's experiment began in his native England, where he was jailed for practicing his Quaker faith. Religious and political freedom were rare in seventeenth-century Europe, and Penn knew firsthand the harsh penalty for straying from state-sanctioned beliefs. In his jail cell, he envisioned a place where people of different religions and origins could live together peacefully.

In 1681, King Charles II handed Penn the means to launch his Holy Experiment when he granted him sixteen million acres of land in the New World to repay a debt owed Penn's deceased father. From the start, Penn made it known that Pennsylvania, named in honor of his father, would be a haven for people of diverse ethnic backgrounds and religious creeds. Word of the tolerant colony spread throughout western Europe, and Conrad Beissel and his followers were among those who sought refuge here.

The wooden doorway to the sisters' house at the cloister is low, and I bow my head to pass through. Historians believe the small entrance is intentional, the tour guide tells us. It teaches humility by keeping those who enter from holding their heads too high. Inside is a sparsely furnished central kitchen, flanked by two workrooms where the sisters met for daily chores.

Each day began at 5 A.M., and the sisters spent their time in the workroom: spinning wool, drawing, sewing, singing. Some pursued

Bethlehem's oldest Moravian church

basket making, gardening, or the fine art of illuminating manuscripts. At 6 P.M., they ate their only hot meal, which one visitor described as "pumpkin mush, with slices of small crusted bread." After dinner, the sisters studied, read, or wrote hymns. They retired at 9 P.M., to be wakened by a bell that tolled each midnight, calling them to devotion. For the next two hours, they worshiped together, then returned to their sleeping cells for three more hours of rest before rising again at 5 A.M.

We walk single file down a narrow hallway to glimpse a typical sleeping cell. Like the doorways, the hallway is confining, too, and reportedly reminds those who pass to keep to the strait and narrow path. The sleeping cell is aptly named, for it measures only two paces across by four paces deep and is utterly cheerless. Bed is a bare wooden bench, exactly fifteen inches wide, with a brick-sized wooden block for a pillow.

The window in the cell is small, and I wonder if this, too, was designed to focus the sisters on the inner life, but I find the Ephrata community did not turn its back on outsiders. Travelers were sheltered and fed free of charge, and the communal society was known for its acts of charity. In 1777, the celibate orders transformed several of their buildings into a military hospital to nurse almost two hundred wounded Revolutionary War soldiers.

I feel claustrophobic and breathe a sigh of relief when we step outside. From my world of thick mattresses and upholstered couches, the cloister seems a harsh place. But to the eighteenth-century residents who sang and worshiped here, it was a haven where they could practice religious beliefs denied them in their native land. In their quest for spiritual rather than material goals, they were much like their Mennonite and Amish neighbors. After Beissel's death in 1768, his followers' zeal for self-denial waned, and by 1813 the celibate orders had disappeared. Members of the married congregation continued at Ephrata until 1934.

Returning to the turnpike, I am jolted back to the twentieth century as I jockey for position with tractor-trailers. The view from the front seat of my Honda is much less inviting than it was from the back seat of my parents' station wagon, and the constant pressure of high-speed traffic no longer endears the turnpike to me. When it opened in 1940 as the nation's first limited-access superhighway, the turnpike boasted no intersections, no pedestrians, no traffic lights, and no speed limit. Some travelers still drive as if there were no speed limit. About three hundred thousand vehicles now travel the turnpike's 506 miles daily, and I think they are all on my tail today.

After passing exits to Hershey, where chocolate perfumes the air, and Harrisburg, the state capital, I cross the wide Susquehanna River and turn off at Exit 17. I head south on the Gettysburg Pike, pass a sign for the Historical Society's Pig Roast and soon reach Pennsylvania's "Apple Country." Although the commonwealth is known for its strong industrial base, its number one "industry" is agriculture, and in Adams County that means twenty thousand acres of fruit trees. In late April and early May, the hills of Adams and neighboring York and Franklin counties are frosted with pink and white blossoms in a spectacle almost too beautiful to be real. Now the harvest is in full swing, and the short, gnarled apple trees are thick with ripe fruit. Wooden crates stamped with each orchard's name are scattered about for migrant pickers to fill.

I turn northwest onto Route 94, pass through the quiet town of York Springs, and suddenly the road buckles into a sea of tall, narrow hills. Orchards surround me, and I slow down at the crest of each hill to admire the rolling countryside before heading into another trough. I pull off at the Peters Orchards, a large fruit stand abundantly stocked with the season's harvest. Alongside traditional varieties— like Jonathan, McIntosh, and Red Delicious—sit baskets of Spartans,

Gettysburg National Military Park

Spigolds, Summer Rambos, and Winter Banana apples. The sweet, musky scent of apples fills the air as I study the produce board on the back wall. Between June 4, when the first Robinson strawberries ripen, and October 30, when York Imperial apples are harvested, the Peters sell sixty-three varieties of fruit.

I find John R. Peters, a young man whose great-grandfather worked this same orchard in the early 1900s, driving a forklift behind the stand. He stops to talk about all the varieties of apples they sell. Gala and Empire are popular varieties now, he says, "but you have to be something of a prophet in the apple business. It's not like the retail business where you can have a bad season and start over the next. When a grower plants an orchard, he is making a thirty-year investment." Some of the Peters trees are still producing after fifty years. I wonder how the apple growers know which variety the public will favor next year—or thirty years from now—as I head south with a jar of apple butter to Gettysburg.

The Civil War was fought in at least a thousand places, but the greatest single battle of the war was waged in the open fields and rolling hills surrounding Gettysburg. For three days in July 1863, more than 160 thousand Union and Confederate troops pummeled each other in a series of brutal engagements that left 51 thousand casualties and played a major role in the outcome of the war. I have never been to Gettysburg but have long wanted to see the battlefield that helped decide the course of our nation's history.

In this small town just north of the Mason-Dixon line, signs of the Civil War and the tourist industry it has spawned are everywhere. I pass the Gettysburg Battle Theatre, General Lee's Family Restaurant, the National Civil War Wax Museum, and an army of family motels. I have been told the best way to see Gettysburg is with a licensed battlefield guide, so the next morning I sign up for one. With time to spare, I poke around the visitor center. Glass cases filled with old canteens, cannonballs, worn leather boots, rifles, and swords line the walls. The wool blue and gray uniforms on display look terribly warm and impractical for Pennsylvania's hot and humid July weather. For years after the war, veterans of the conflict continued to wear these uniforms when they gathered at reunions.

Leaving these old war relics, I cross the street to the national cemetery, where over five thousand Union soldiers are buried. Near the Lincoln Speech Memorial, I join a tour led by Stephanie Wortz, a costumed living-history interpreter, who is portraying Effie Goldsborough. A young Baltimore woman whose family supported the Confederacy, Effie arrived in Gettysburg nine days after the battle to help tend the thousands of wounded men left in the townspeople's care. She tried to help one soldier with a chest wound keep upright and able to breathe by sitting all night long with her back tied to his. Although she nursed both Union and Confederate soldiers, Effie admits she was partial to one rebel who eventually died of his wounds.

Effie's story is not unique. Many thousands of women helped the Civil War effort. In the North, women sewed, knit, wrapped bandages, baked, and raised funds for the soldiers. Clara Barton dispensed supplies to the fighting men by mule train. Southern women transformed their homes into hospitals.

As Effie spins her tale, a man in our group falls unconscious to the ground. Stephanie snaps out of character and asks someone to run for help. Three of us take off for the visitor center. By the time we return, the man is sitting up, and an ambulance soon arrives. But I feel unnerved by this talk of war casualties and leave the cemetery to rejoin the land of the living for a late lunch before touring the battlefield.

I meet my guide, Mark Troup, at the appointed hour, and together with a couple from Colorado, we relive the Battle of Gettysburg. We

Bedford County Courthouse

stand on McPherson Ridge where John Buford's cavalry dismounted to fight a much larger force of Confederate infantry. On Route 30, we pass a marker where the first man fell. With more than thirteen hundred monuments scattered throughout the park, this is a much commemorated battle.

We drive by rows of cannons and stop to feel the spiral grooves inside one to understand how this rifling helped the cannon fire accurately. Civil War battlefields were noisy, smoky places, and the weapons often proved cumbersome. It took nine men to operate one cannon, and the best-drilled artillery crews could fire their weapons only four times a minute. On Little Round Top, we peer into the rocky thicket where Joshua Lawrence Chamberlain, his troops almost out of ammunition, led a daring bayonet charge that overwhelmed the exhausted rebels and held the Union line. Chamberlain was later elected governor of Maine.

We also stare across the field where General George Pickett, under Robert E. Lee's battle plan, led his disastrous charge at the Union center. Only about one-third of the twelve thousand Confederates who marched out across this field returned safely, and once Pickett's Charge was repulsed, the Battle of Gettysburg was over. After a series of stunning victories, General Lee was stopped at Gettysburg. The Confederates marched into Pennsylvania, hoping to end the war, and retreated with the tide turned against them.

As I leave Gettysburg, it seems the battle has just ended. I head west on the old Lincoln Highway and think of Abraham Lincoln's healing words, delivered at the dedication of Gettysburg National Cemetery: ". . . that we here highly resolve that these dead shall not have died in vain—that this nation, under God, shall have a new birth of freedom—and that, government of the people, by the people, for the people, shall not perish from the earth." The nation did not perish,

and the wounds that divided our country slowly began to heal. At the seventy-fifth reunion of the Blue and the Gray in 1938, more than eighteen hundred Civil War veterans, some past one hundred years old, gathered at Gettysburg to dedicate a monument to "Peace Eternal in a Nation United."

The sun starts to sink as I drive west into the Laurel Highlands, a region extending from southcentral to southwestern Pennsylvania, where mountain laurel, the state flower, blooms in white and pale-pink profusion each June. I pass Chambersburg and McConnellsburg, where antique tractors parade up the main street each fall, then push on to Breezewood. After dark, I leave Route 30 for the lights of the turnpike and drive west to Bedford for a night's sleep.

The Bedford exit of the turnpike is paved with fast-food restaurants, family motels, and gas stations, but if you head south on Business 220 and turn right at the covered bridge, the twentieth century disappears at Old Bedford Village. The covered bridge was not built here; it was moved here piece by numbered piece, along with over forty other structures built between 1750 and 1850 in Bedford County. Log, brick, and stone buildings, once miles apart, are neighbors now along the main street of this reconstructed pioneer village.

A wisp of smoke curls from the chimney of the Kegg-Blasko House, a two-story log home near the entrance to the village. As I step out of a cold autumn rain, the warm fire inside draws me to Susan Ferguson, who is stirring a pot of potato soup on the open hearth. Like all the guides and craftsmen in the village, she wears the unadorned dress of Pennsylvania's early settlers. Her gray cotton gown, dust cap, and apron are all handmade by village workers. The house is simply furnished, too, but Susan admits the glass windows and wood floors—both luxuries for the pioneers—were probably added later. There are cracks between the floorboards in the second story above, and I imagine

Bland's Park near Altoona

this cozy log home could have been quite drafty with only wooden shutters to keep out the cold.

The main street of Old Bedford Village takes me back to an era when blacksmiths, candlemakers, and tinsmiths plied their trades; when apothecaries dispensed rosemary for headaches; and when families sat around a hearth, not a television set. In the dollmaker's shop, which is fragrant with drying herbs, Jean Senne appreciates this difference. She spends part of every week living in a small apartment above one of the village's historic buildings. With no television or telephone and only a hot plate for cooking, she is perfectly content. "It's wonderful here," says Jean, her eyes sparkling beneath tight brown curls. "It's so quiet. I like the quiet. You can think." Jean is learning to use herbs from the village garden in her crafts, and the village basket maker is teaching her—with great patience, she insists—to weave baskets.

In the woodworking shop, a tall, graying man stoops over his workbench sanding a piece of wood, which he tells me will become the neck of a banjo. Like many of the craftsmen here, Cork Wirick is pursuing in his retirement something he loves. He builds most of his banjos in the privacy of his own workshop, but one day a week he comes to Old Bedford Village to show others how to make a piece of wood sing.

Cork grew up just across the ridge from the village but took a forty-year detour to pursue a banking career in Florida before returning to the hills where he was born. "Moving back here was like moving back in time," he says. He shows me the ebony fingerboard of a finished banjo in which he has inlaid mother of pearl. "It takes me ninety hours to make one. I should quit shooting for perfection and start shooting for excellence," he chuckles. Cork makes eight to ten instruments a year. "I don't hurry them. I just like to do it."

I wonder aloud how the banjo with the ebony fingerboard sounds, and he plays the theme from "The Beverly Hillbillies." I always thought Appalachia and hillbillies belonged to the South. But the twang of his banjo reminds me that the Allegheny Mountains, which run through Bedford County and northeast across Pennsylvania, are part of the ancient Appalachian chain.

The frontier life, which is now re-created in Old Bedford Village, began to disappear with the coming of the railroad and the gathering force of the Industrial Revolution. In the mid-1800s, the adoption of coke in ironmaking transformed southwestern Pennsylvania into one of the world's foremost centers for the making of iron and steel. The huge deposits of bituminous, or soft coal, that stretched across this mountainous region could easily be refined into coke. As the mines and mills sprang up, the Pennsylvania Railroad expanded its influence by linking them to their markets.

I leave the pioneers of Old Bedford Village and head north on Route 220 to Altoona, a town virtually built by the Pennsylvania Railroad. My route winds between two ridges of the Alleghenies, and it becomes clear why these mountains once impeded east-west travel.

In the 1700s, it took nearly three weeks for wagons to haul freight the three hundred miles between Philadelphia and Pittsburgh. In 1834, travel time was cut to four and a half days with the opening of the Allegheny Portage Railroad and Pennsylvania Main Line Canal, which relied on a series of trains, canals, and inclined planes to cross the Alleghenies. Charles Dickens crossed Pennsylvania by this ingenious means in 1842, but the canals were unreliable: they froze in winter, dried up when rain was scarce, and constantly needed to be cleared of debris. An all-rail route was essential, and with the completion of the Horseshoe Curve in 1854, travel between east and west opened up.

An engineering marvel of its day, the Horseshoe Curve overcame the steep grade of the Alleghenies by sending trains on a U-shaped bend through the mountains above Altoona. It was constructed by 450

GE locomotive construction in Erie

imported Irish laborers with picks, shovels, powder, and mules. For each twelve-hour day of backbreaking work, the men earned 25 cents. When it was new, people used to ride the train just to pass through the curve, which cut travel time between Philadelphia and Pittsburgh to thirteen hours. During World War II, the curve burst into prominence again when it was targeted by Nazi saboteurs, who were caught before disrupting its steady stream of supply and troop trains.

Born after the golden age of the Pennsylvania Railroad, I find it hard to imagine the power the "Pennsy" once held. At its height in the early decades of this century, "the Standard Railroad of the World," as it billed itself, employed 280 thousand people, and its enormous shops sprawled over seven miles of Altoona. Close to seven thousand locomotives were built here, and the tracks crisscrossing Altoona could handle seventeen thousand freight cars at one time. The Pennsylvania Railroad ceased to exist after a disastrous 1968 merger with its longtime rival the New York Central. The Penn Central soon went bankrupt, but its successor, Conrail, still pulls freight trains through Altoona. I hope to glimpse one rounding the Horseshoe Curve today.

Rain beats on my windshield as I head up the winding road leading to the curve, and although my route parallels it, the curve is not visible. At the lookout above the visitor center, I can finally see the U-shaped tracks as they loop around the valley. By now, rain is falling sideways, and I try to keep dry beneath a small platform. Wind whips through the trees on the nearby hillsides, knocking leaves down helter-skelter. I talk briefly with the one other person, a man from Virginia, who is waiting, too. When I tell him I have been to Gettysburg, he says, "Bobby Lee really blew it there." I wonder at the familiar way he speaks of this courtly southern general, and suddenly I feel like a Yankee.

We fall silent again, waiting, until I think I hear a droning in the distance. It soon grows to a rumbling, and seven blue Conrail engines appear, pulling a freight train up the hill. As the cars grow closer, I no longer hear the wind, only the incessant roar of the engines and the mournful blast of the whistle. The train rounds the bend with a great screeching and grinding of metal wheels on metal rails.

A kid again, I wave to the engineer and revel in the train's deafening roar. For a moment, I am part of the curve and the train as it wraps around the valley. The cars keep coming and coming, until the train stretches the entire length of the curve. I watch, wanting to hop aboard to see where this powerful force will take me. I lose sight of the engines as they leave the valley, and my eyes follow the final string of freight cars around the bend and into the distance until the last have vanished. Then I notice the wind and rain again and am ready to return to my Honda.

The next morning I head west on Route 22 and watch, with new appreciation, as a freight train snakes along the mountain beside me. Near Ebensburg, I pick up Route 219 South and am so distracted by the hardwoods that have turned yellow during the past few cold nights that I nearly miss my exit for St. Michael. In the 1880s, the great industrialists of the day—men such as Andrew Mellon, Andrew Carnegie, and Henry Clay Frick—retreated to St. Michael with their families to fish and boat on Lake Conemaugh. They came as members of the South Fork Fishing and Hunting Club, a private summer resort for Pittsburgh's wealthy elite. I am looking for traces of the club and lake that no longer exist.

As I enter St. Michael, I expect to see a row of Victorian cottages along a dry lake bed, but what I find is a coal-mining town and a man intent on preserving its past. Walter Costlow is a solid man with a sense of purpose, and I am not surprised when he tells me he spent a career in the military. Born and raised in St. Michael, he could have followed his father into the coal mines, but in high school, after a trip into the mine, he decided there had to be "an easier way to make a living." The day

Miners National Bank in Pottsville

after graduation, he joined the Marines. "I had no intentions of ever being back here," says Walter, but after retiring in 1986, he returned home and "found it's a pretty nice place to be."

As we drive around St. Michael, Walter points to rows of cookie-cutter houses. In 1903, the Berwind White Coal Company started digging a bituminous mine shaft above the old South Fork cottages. It built a company town, like many others in southwestern Pennsylvania, complete with its own bank and store. "This was a very picturesque town," says Walter. "It had walks. It had fenced yards. Talk about a socialistic program, you had birth-to-death benefits. . . . The people who worked for the Berwind White Company worked for the best coal company in the business. They were fifty years ahead of anybody else in their management."

The coal company considered different ethnic groups better qualified for different jobs, Walter says, "so we had Italians and Slovenians and Hungarians and Polish and Germans and Welsh and British and French, and they all lived in this town. The northern Italians were considered the best tipple men, and the Welsh were considered the best coal managers." I think again of Penn's Holy Experiment and believe St. Michael's ethnic mix would have pleased him.

When the mine closed in 1958, St. Michael's fortunes began to decline. The company painters no longer brushed a fresh coat of gray or yellow or green paint on the homes, and when a picket in your fence broke, the mine office no longer sent a carpenter to repair it. But St. Michael had something other mining towns lacked, and that brings Walter and me back to the town's Victorian past.

Walter stops the car in front of a white clapboard home with red shutters and an inviting front porch. He now lives in this four-bedroom house, but in the days of the South Fork Fishing and Hunting Club, Andrew Mellon reportedly slept here. Of the club's sixteen original buildings, eight survive, and Walter has spearheaded a movement to preserve them. We drive up to the old clubhouse, where most members stayed and all ate their meals, according to club rules. The wraparound porch is freshly painted, but otherwise the exterior needs repair.

Inside the clubhouse, where the titans of Pittsburgh society once dined and forged business deals, we enter a dimly lit meeting room with worn red carpeting. A honky-tonk bar occupies another corner of this large frame building, but most rooms are vacant. Dark paneling covers the old wallpaper, and the stairs creak ominously as we climb them.

Upstairs I see what looks like a rundown boarding house, the rooms in disarray and slowly decaying. Walter sees something different. If all goes according to plan, the years of neglect will be gutted and a completely renovated, full-service hotel will open here. When it is restored, the guests most likely will come because nearly two hundred thousand people visit St. Michael each year. They come not to see a coal-mining town but to contemplate a dry lake bed and the terrible flood unleashed here on Johnstown in 1889.

Walter describes some recently discovered photographs of the South Fork Fishing and Hunting Club. In one, a young boy dives from a board balanced on a sawhorse. In another, fashionable young women in long dresses boat on Lake Conemaugh. When I see these photographs later, the subjects seem oblivious to the danger they would face should the board shift or the boat topple, and I suspect most of the club members never thought about the safety of the earthen dam that supported the lake's twenty million tons of water.

The South Fork Dam, which created Lake Conemaugh, was built in 1853 to supply water to the Pennsylvania Main Line Canal. It was soon abandoned along with the canal system, and by the time the South Fork Club bought it in 1879, it needed repairs. The Club carelessly patched the dam, but the heavy rains of May 1889 precipitated a disaster.

Holsteins at Vista Grande Farm

On May 30, a storm blew in from the Midwest. By the next morning, the lake behind the dam was filling at the alarming rate of one inch every ten minutes. Elias Unger, the club's president, directed workers to dig another spillway and try to raise the dam. But the water rose too quickly, and at 3:10 P.M., club engineer John Parke wrote in his diary, "the fearful rushing waters opened the gap with such increasing rapidity that soon after the entire lake leaped out."

A crushing wall of water burst down the Little Conemaugh Valley, obliterating everything in its path. Houses broke like eggshells, trees snapped in two, and even locomotives were hurled toward Johnstown. Before the dam gave way, Parke tried to warn the residents in the towns downstream, but the message never reached Johnstown, fourteen miles away. A "roar like thunder" preceded the thirty-six-foot wall of water and debris, which exploded into Johnstown at 4:07 P.M.

When the wave hit Johnstown, a booming steel town of thirty thousand, the streets "grew black with people running for their lives," wrote an observer. In many buildings, water rose to the third story. Thousands of people clung to roofs, boards, and other pieces of debris as the water swept them along. The terrifying ride ended at the stone railroad bridge across the Conemaugh River where tons of rubble and hundreds of people piled up, some entangled in the miles of barbed wire that washed down when the wave destroyed the wireworks.

To compound the tragedy, the oil-soaked mass trapped by the bridge caught fire, killing eighty people at the bridge, some still in their own homes. "One horror I will never forget," wrote a survivor, "people dying first by water then by fire." In less than ten minutes, four square miles of downtown Johnstown were demolished.

Over twenty-two hundred people lost their lives in the one frantic hour it took the water to thunder down the river valley and sweep over Johnstown. The flood wiped out ninety-nine entire families, orphaned ninety-eight children, and left thousands homeless. More than a century later, the Johnstown Flood remains one of Pennsylvania's worst tragedies, but what is most remarkable is the flood's aftermath. Within hours of the disaster, survivors had called meetings, formed work crews, established a hospital, and begun digging out from the wreckage.

Press accounts of the deadliest flood in American history prompted an outpouring of volunteers and over $3.7 million in aid. People sent mattresses, stoves, combs, and more than seven thousand pairs of shoes. Clara Barton and her newly formed Red Cross arrived five days after the disaster and spent the next five months tending the injured and homeless. Johnstown's main employer, the Cambria Iron Company, withstood the flood, and within days, the men reported for work and fired the furnaces again. Some of the survivors left, but many stayed and rebuilt their lives.

The members of the South Fork Fishing and Hunting Club did not return. Reviled in the press, the lake gone, they abandoned their mountain retreat. I leave Walter Costlow on the outskirts of St. Michael at the Johnstown Flood National Memorial, where he volunteers, and drive to the south abutment of the old South Fork Dam. A railroad track and river wind through the lush green meadow that has grown over the old lake bed, and a few trees have taken root. The lake bed has recovered, like Johnstown itself, but the flood changed both forever.

From St. Michael, I head into Johnstown for a ride up the incline built after the flood to shuttle workers from the valley below to new housing above the flood plain. From the top of the incline, the bustling city below reveals no trace of its tragic past, but on a nearby hillside, over 750 white marble headstones mark the graves of the flood's unknown victims. I leave this valley that has seen the best of times and the worst of times and head south to Route 30, which takes me west to Pittsburgh.

Carnegie Mellon's robotics research

My youngest sister settled in Pittsburgh after attending Carnegie Mellon University here, and during my visits over the years, I have come to admire this city of bridges, tunnels, and neighborhoods built on steep hills. The next day I drive to the Strip District, Pittsburgh's wholesale shopping area. In early morning the district bustles with activity. Drivers unload truckloads of fresh seafood, meat, and produce to stock the shops for the bargain hunters along Penn Avenue. Merchants here do not cater to fast-food tastes but sell fresh fruits and vegetables and a richly varied international fare: croissants, Peking duck, feta cheese, espresso.

Many groups that settled in Pittsburgh have maintained their ethnic identities in neighborhoods separated by the hilly topography. Here in the Strip District, they come together for a taste of the old country. At the Pennsylvania Macaroni Company, where clerks slice wedges from huge rounds of Italian cheese, I count more than twenty types of olive oil and discover varieties of pasta, like cavatappi and mezzi tubetti, I never knew existed.

As I walk from shop to shop, the merchandise sometimes spilling outside onto the sidewalk, I revel in colorful bouquets of chrysanthemums and luscious fruit tortes. Produce stalls brim with fresh green beans, carrots, and tomatoes. This is honest-to-goodness food that stands on its own merits without fancy surroundings or marketing gimmicks. At a luncheonette, I order a bowl of thick vegetable soup that comes with two enormous slices of crusty Italian bread. It is delicious!

After lunch, I follow the Monongahela River east to Braddock and the Edgar Thomson Plant, Andrew Carnegie's first steel mill. Blast furnaces once glowed red all across Pittsburgh's night sky, but during the 1970s and 1980s, Indiana and Illinois became the major center of the domestic steel industry, ending Pittsburgh's reign as the "Steel City."

Service industries—such as health care and high technology—have supplanted steel in economic importance, but the steelworker is still woven into the fabric of this city, and I want to visit this icon of Pittsburgh's industrial might.

When you reach Braddock, you cannot miss the miles of chain link fence that encircle the huge steel mill. Once inside, I am issued a protective shirt and pants, which I slip over street clothes, along with a hard hat, goggles, and ear plugs. My escort, Frank Davis, leads me to Manny Stoupis, a process and inventory manager, who first reported for work here in 1959. When Manny began his career in steel, fresh out of college, twenty-seven blast furnaces burned in the Monongahela Valley; only two remain today, both at Edgar Thomson. "I've worked at every blast furnace plant in the Mon Valley," Manny tells me. He left Edgar Thomson in 1964 for a job at another mill. Over the years, he moved from mill to mill. The furnaces closed one by one, and eventually the plants themselves shut down. "Everyplace I go closes down. I have quite a reputation," he laughs.

Manny managed to support his six children, but thousands of other steelworkers lost their jobs in the early eighties when most of the big mills shut down. "There was such confusion, there was such hysteria," says Manny, his brow furrowed. The valley lost a lot of its skilled labor when many workers accepted a buyout option and moved elsewhere.

It was a wrenching time. "All of my fifty-some years have been in the steel mill. My brothers, my cousins . . . all of my family has been in steel since I don't known when. Really, if that's all you've known, I think it's difficult for anybody to find another way of life. . . . It wasn't an easy situation."

After years of decline, Manny believes Pittsburgh's steel industry is growing stronger. The Edgar Thomson plant is humming with orders, and profits are up. In recent years, productivity and quality have both

Liver-transplant pioneer Dr. Starzl

dramatically improved. Stiff foreign competition and the loss of jobs have propelled these changes. "I think we all realize that, hey, if it falls on its face here," he pauses, "there's nothing. We can't all flip hamburgers, you know."

I like Manny's straight talk and lack of pretension. He appears genuine, much like the goods at the Strip District. He does not use packaged techniques to manage his people; instead, he relies on his own sense of ethics and fair play. Steel is clearly more than a job for Manny, and the bottom line, while obviously important, is not the only motivating factor. "You treat people right, you're remembered," he tells me before we part. "And that's the important consideration. You leave here, you don't leave much. All this is gone. But you leave your name, and I think you leave the way you treat people."

The roar of the mill outside Manny's office is deafening. I put in my earplugs as Frank Davis leads me along a series of catwalks past a maze of metal ducts, tanks, and scaffolding to the blast furnace, which stands five stories high. The acrid smell of sulphur rises from huge slag piles being hosed down in the distance. We pass a pile of rubble where Blast Furnace Number Two once roared. Steam hisses around us as a "skip" dumps its load with a thundering crash into the bowels of the blast furnace.

Through the protective glass of the control room, I watch an ironworker take a sample for the lab from the glowing yellow iron flowing like lava out of the furnace. The impurities, or slag, run down a different channel. The worker is dressed like a spaceman in a reflective suit to protect against the 2,700° Fahrenheit heat. Sparks fly, and a fine dust rises from the molten iron. The work demands intense concentration because making iron and steel can be dangerous.

Since Andrew Carnegie opened this plant in 1875, steelmaking has seen changes. Computers now regulate production, and pollution control devices keep the air clean. But at its heart, it is still men working in a fiery universe to meet the demands of an industrial world.

I leave Braddock for a ride up Mount Washington and a view of the Pittsburgh skyline. The glass-and-steel skyscrapers turn orange in the setting sun, and the city glows much like the furnaces I have just left. Here at the Golden Triangle, where the Allegheny and Monongahela rivers flow together to form the Ohio, is Pittsburgh's sparkling downtown: a city of corporate headquarters, a home of great universities, a leader in health care. Here, Dr. Jonas Salk invented the polio vaccine, and Dr. Thomas Starzl performed groundbreaking liver transplants. Here, the great industrialists left a legacy of cultural institutions: the Carnegie with its library, Dinosaur Hall, and art museum; the Phipps Conservatory; the Heinz Hall for the Performing Arts. Here is one of the world's largest inland ports, and one of the safest cities of its size in the nation.

The city was not always so pretty. During the early decades of the twentieth century, a thick veil of smoke hung in the air, and streetlights remained lit twenty-four hours a day. In a 1936 photograph taken by photojournalist Margaret Bourke-White, Pittsburgh looks smoky and charred, as if burned in a great fire. After World War II—like the mythical phoenix that rose from the ashes—Pittsburgh, tired of its sooty image, reinvented itself. A new downtown skyline rose, and heavy industries were allowed to pollute no more. Like Johnstown, the city experienced a remarkable comeback.

In the evening, I watch the city lights twinkle across the Monongahela from my dinner table in the Grand Concourse, an elegant old building that once served as the terminal for the Pittsburgh & Lake Erie Railroad. The restaurant is filled with men and women in business attire, and the air is charged with a feeling of material well-being. Next door, developers have transformed the old railroad warehouses into Station Square,

Pittsburgh's beloved Fred Rogers

a collection of restaurants and upscale shops where I browse after dinner. In these comfortable surroundings, Pittsburgh seems a city of possibilities, a place where people have learned to create a better future by building—and sometimes improving—on their past.

The next morning, I reluctantly leave Pennsylvania's "Gateway to the West" and drive north on Route 28 through rolling countryside. Sunlight streams through puffy clouds spotlighting huge, round bales of hay in freshly mown fields. I pass Moose lodges and fire halls in quiet towns such as New Bethlehem, Mahoning Furnace, or Distant—a name that suits this remote hamlet. Logging trucks rumble by with their precious cargo. Ahead lies the Allegheny National Forest, with more than five hundred thousand acres of wooded land and some of the most valuable black cherry and oak timber in the world.

When the Allegheny became a national forest in 1923, it looked more like a brushpatch than a woodland. The virgin forests of white pine, hemlock, maple, ash, and oak that blanketed the state when William Penn arrived in 1682 had nearly vanished. They were stripped by settlers who planted crops, lumber barons who fed the growing nation's ravenous appetite for wood, and industrialists who fueled foundries and built mine shafts with the timber.

As the forests fell, the rich woodlands became barren wasteland. In 1898, the state government began buying up the spent land and established a system of parks and forests that served as a model for other states. About the same time, the federal government began to develop its own system of forest reserves, where logging would be regulated, and the Allegheny became Pennsylvania's only national forest.

My destination is Cook Forest State Park, just south of the national forest. Despite heavy logging and forest fires over the years, the park shelters one of the largest stands of virgin white pine and hemlock in the state. I stop for lunch in Brookville, a county seat protective of its Victorian heritage. Brookville's wide Main Street with its old-fashioned storefronts is dominated by a massive red-brick courthouse. It reminds me of other thriving small towns—such as Ligonier, Jim Thorpe, and Lititz—sprinkled like jewels across the commonwealth.

From Brookville, I meander up Route 36 past fields of bright orange pumpkins to Cook Forest and a comfortable lodge along the Clarion River. Long ago, the Senecas left their carvings in boulders by this river's shore. I lace up hiking boots and climb the park's fire tower for a view from above the timberline. Beneath me, spreading in every direction, are thousands of trees, some still in their summer green, others wearing colorful new fall robes. In the distance, the river snakes through the wooded valley. This must have been the way Pennsylvania, or "Penn's Woods," looked to William Penn—a boundless wilderness, a land of abundant natural wealth.

Wishing to explore this great forest, I decide to hike the Longfellow Trail, which winds up a hill into a cool, moist world of ancient hemlock and white pine. The earth is soft and damp beneath my feet, and I jump over several springs that wash across the trail. I meet no one except a father and his boys wandering through the forest. This is a shadowy world; the treetops towering two hundred feet above me drink in the sunlight before it can filter down to the moss-covered forest floor. I try to wrap my arms around the rough, brown bark of one of these giants but can encircle only half its girth.

I reach the Forest Cathedral, a national natural landmark, where some of these same trees stood over two hundred years ago. Storms have uprooted a number of these natural treasures, but even in decay they continue to nourish the earth. As I stand in the middle of this forest primeval, surrounded by a state of almost twelve million people, I am completely alone. In the northern tier of Pennsylvania, there are still places where you can fish or hike or simply daydream in total solitude.

Presque Isle State Park near Erie

The next morning, I retrace my route to Brookville and I-80. With more time, I would have driven northwest to Titusville, where Edwin Drake drilled the world's first commercial oil well, and continued on to Erie. The grape harvest is underway, and thousands of birds are migrating through Presque Isle State Park. The beaches of Presque Isle, a sandy finger of land that juts seven miles into Lake Erie, draw more than four million visitors a year and boast some of the most beautiful sunsets in the world. It is hard to believe this lake was so polluted in the 1960s that people proclaimed it dead. Massive clean-up efforts rejuvenated it, and like Pittsburgh, it sparkles again.

I drive east on I-80, then south into Centre County, the geographic center of the state and home to picturesque dairy farms and the Pennsylvania State University. With nearly thirty-eight thousand full-time students at its main campus, Penn State dominates life in State College. The upscale stores along College Avenue cater to both the young and professional communities, and the Penn State Nittany Lions are everywhere—on tee shirts, mugs, books, hats, you name it. Football is king here, and Penn State fans are loyal subjects: they crowd Beaver Stadium's ninety-three thousand seats in rain, shine, or snow. For tomorrow's game against the Maryland Terrapins, the candy store is featuring chocolate turtles. Presumably you can swallow the opponent whole while cheering on the home team.

This weekend, the football squad is away, but the over-forty set has descended on campus for parents weekend. As I walk the tree-lined paths to Old Main, I see the embarrassment of one young woman who keeps three paces ahead of her parents and younger brother. The next morning, while I savor my "grilled sticky," a deliciously gooey cinnamon bun, at Ye Olde College Diner, the booths are filled with students and parents catching up with each other. When I leave the Happy Valley, I think about this university that began as an agricultural

school in the heart of Pennsylvania. Since its founding in 1855, the school's mission and influence have grown. One in every seven hundred Americans is a Penn State graduate, according to the university's alumni association. No wonder I spot so many Penn State bumper stickers on the highways.

Clouds darken the sky as I head north, and by the time I reach Woolrich, it is drizzling. Pennsylvania averages forty-one inches of precipitation a year, and most of it seems to be falling during this trip. It has not discouraged the Saturday shoppers converging on this "one-mill town" to stock up on the outdoor clothing and woolen goods, including the signature red-and-black Buffalo plaid, which is manufactured here. Since 1830, seven generations of the Rich family have been involved in Woolrich. Like several other successful Pennsylvania companies—such as Martin Guitar, Pfaltzgraff (pottery), and Yuengling Brewery—Woolrich has prospered for more than a century and a half under family ownership.

Fog enshrouds Route 15, and I creep north in a blinding rain to Mansfield and the overstuffed Victorian comfort of Nelle and Clancy Prevost's bed-and-breakfast. Clancy grew up in nearby Wellsboro, but left town to become a commercial airline pilot and marry Nelle, a flight attendant. In 1987, they were living in Dallas and starting to mull over retirement when they returned to his hometown for a visit. Clancy warned Nelle to "be careful or you'll fall in love with this place." Two days later, on a whim, they bought a sprawling white clapboard home above Wellsboro's wide boulevard lined with gas lamps, and moved here.

"Nothing ever changes in Wellsboro," says Clancy. "You could set your clock back forty years—that's how little the town has changed." Everybody knows everybody here, and Clancy finds "there's a lot of continuity in a place like this." When the Prevosts bought the

John Rich VI of Woolrich

bed-and-breakfast in Mansfield, they continued a family tradition; an earlier Prevost opened an inn nearby in 1814.

Tradition and family heritage are important in the small towns across this state. Clancy's ancestor, Cecelia Le Fevre, came to northern Pennsylvania in 1792 to escape the French Revolution. She was among the émigrés who settled at the French Azilum, a refuge along the Susquehanna River some say was built for Marie Antoinette. The French queen, of course, died on the guillotine, but Cecelia remained, married John Prevost, and helped to settle the wilderness.

When Clancy's ancestors first arrived in northern Pennsylvania, elk herds grazed in the river valleys, panthers and wolves roamed the forests, and eagles soared above the thick canopy of trees. The dense woodlands and the abundant wildlife they sustained fell victim to voracious lumbering and unregulated hunting in the 1800s. But west of Wellsboro, I visit a place that remembers those days.

Like its larger western cousin, the rocky walls of the "Grand Canyon of Pennsylvania" recall the land before time. Pine Creek winds through this gorge, cutting a channel up to 1,450 feet deep into almost four hundred million years of geologic history. Marine fossils embedded near the bottom of the gorge reveal that the land was once submerged beneath the sea. Glacial meltwater carved the canyon during the Pleistocene Ice Age, which released its frigid grip on northern Pennsylvania thirteen thousand years ago.

I follow the popular Turkey Path, once an old mule drag used for logging, down into the gorge. With fall foliage nearing its peak, I pass many hikers who stop to catch their breath on wooden landings built into the steepest parts of the trail. At the bottom, I sit on a gray boulder partly submerged in Pine Creek. When the first white men explored the gorge, they "found as many as thirty rattlesnakes lying on a rock, sunning themselves," according to Pine Creek pioneer Phillip Tome.

I see no snakes here but feel a sense of hope knowing that this stretch of the canyon, once stripped of its forests, is now protected by the state. Eagles and ospreys have returned, and river otters again splash in its cool waters.

Leaving the picnickers at the top of the canyon, I retrace my way east on Route 6, a scenic highway that curves past century-old farmhouses and cornfields. In these quiet hills known as the Endless Mountains, you can still hear old-time fiddling and echoes of the simple tunes Stephen Foster began to compose in nearby Athens. Despite the beauty of its flaming foliage, Route 6 has a darker side—it partly retraces General John Sullivan's march, which opened the area to white settlement in 1779 by destroying forty Indian villages. The good relations William Penn had fostered with the Indians lay in ruins. By the late 1700s, Pennsylvania's original settlers had either left the state or literally disappeared into the hills, often intermarrying or hiding their identity.

In 1984, Carl Wayandaga, a full-blooded Nanticoke who grew up in the Endless Mountains, brought the tribes of Pennsylvania back together. Descendants of the Susquehannock, Lenni-Lenape, Shawnee, and nine other tribes came together as members of the Eastern Delaware Nation and began gathering for powwows in Forksville. It gave them a chance to continue—and in some cases to learn—the traditions of their ancestors.

In Forksville, I meet Ulla Nass, a small woman with long, dark braids, who runs a Native American trading post and has continued Wayandaga's work since his death in 1992. "People like to know where their roots are," she tells me. "The Endless Mountains are as sacred to the Delaware as the Black Hills are to the Sioux." I go to High Knob Overlook in World's End State Park, one of Chief Wayandaga's favorite places, and stand transfixed as the sky turns orange, then purple, over the forested mountains, which do seem to roll endlessly into the distance. After sunset, I head for Eagles Mere, a small town of rambling

Home of Nobel laureate Pearl S. Buck

Victorian homes on a nearby mountaintop. The same families return to this quiet resort town summer after summer to golf or sail or simply enjoy its leisurely pace. Like Wellsboro, it is a "town time forgot."

Next morning, the last of my trip, I head for Ricketts Glen State Park, named for a colonel who fought at Gettysburg and owned eighty thousand acres of land here. Kitchen Creek rushes through two gorges in the park, tumbling down a series of waterfalls before meeting and flowing through a forest of ancient trees, some over five hundred years old. I follow the hypnotic roar of water into Ganoga Glen, past falls with Indian names that remind me of the first people to walk on Pennsylvania soil over twelve thousand years ago. At ninety-four-foot Ganoga Falls, the park's tallest, a fine mist sprays my face as water courses through a narrow channel, then fans out across a series of rocky ledges below.

Water seeps out of gray sandstone outcrops along the trail, making it slick underfoot. Fallen tree trunks, wet to the core, nurture moss and ferns, and colorful lichens cling to the rocks. Yellow beech and maple leaves drift lazily down before being swept away by the current. I stop to rest on a bench where the two branches of Kitchen Creek meet, a national natural landmark. I hear songbirds in the trees and feel at peace in this watery paradise.

But my journey must end, and soon I head south on Route 487 past weathered barns and fields of Christmas trees. I-80 propels me east to the turnpike's northeastern extension and away from the tranquil Endless Mountains. I whiz by the anthracite-coal country and pass turnpike exits for Jim Thorpe—where the Olympic gold medalist is buried—and the industrial cities of Allentown, Bethlehem, and Easton.

In Quakertown, I exit east to Route 309, and as I drive south through Bucks County, I think of the creative spirits this land of stone farmhouses has nourished: James Michener, George Kaufman, Pearl Buck, Oscar Hammerstein. I am in familiar territory now. This southeastern corner of Pennsylvania is where my home and my roots are. My father's father immigrated to Philadelphia in 1927. He spoke no English when he arrived but soon found work as a cabinetmaker. The next year, my father and grandmother made the week-long journey across the sea—hoping to escape Germany's spiraling inflation and begin a better life here.

My grandparents were like hundreds of thousands of other immigrants who flowed into Pennsylvania—from the earliest Dutch and Swedish settlers to the most recent Asian—looking for religious and political freedom or economic opportunity. Philadelphia and its suburbs now sprawl across eight Pennsylvania and New Jersey counties, and with 5.8 million people, it is America's fourth-largest metropolitan area.

When William Penn laid out the City of Brotherly Love, he proposed an orderly grid of straight streets, and suggested that homeowners build in the middle of their lots to allow room for gardens so "that it may be a green country town, which will never be burnt and always be wholesome." Trees still line many Philadelphia streets with names like Walnut, Locust, and Pine, and the city's eighty-seven-hundred-acre Fairmount Park is the largest landscaped urban park in the world.

My route into downtown Philadelphia cuts through Fairmount Park and skirts the shores of the Schuylkill River, where Japanese cherry trees explode with pink blossoms each spring. In the golden light of early morning, the river and the scullers that ply its waters look much the way Thomas Eakins painted them over a century ago. The river drive leads past Boathouse Row to the broad Benjamin Franklin Parkway, home to a number of museums, including the Philadelphia Museum of Art, the Rodin Museum, and the Franklin Institute Science Museum.

It seems fitting that one of the Institute's most popular exhibits is a walk-through model of the heart, because Benjamin Franklin's heart still beats beneath the surface of the city he helped shape. In our specialized age, the scope of Franklin's achievements is almost unimaginable.

During his lifetime, which spanned most of the eighteenth century, Franklin helped found the city's first hospital, its first circulating library, its first fire company, the American Philosophical Society and the University of Pennsylvania. With only two years of formal schooling and apprenticeships in soap-making and printing, he distinguished himself as a publisher, printer, diplomat, inventor, scientist, and statesman. His presence and the revolutionary times in which he lived are stamped on the stately brick buildings of Independence National Historical Park. The First and Second Continental congresses gathered here, and when the English failed to address their grievances, the Declaration of Independence was adopted here. It is a place—like Valley Forge or Gettysburg—that draws visitors from around the world. Even in the dead of winter, I see tourists bundled in blankets, listening to tour guides driving horse-drawn carriages through the old city.

A few blocks west of Independence Mall, a shining city of modern skyscrapers soars above William Penn's statue on City Hall. On clear autumn evenings, the setting sun bathes these monuments of commerce in orange light, and the skyline sparkles with the promise William Penn could hardly have imagined. In this century, Philadelphia has continued to produce nationally known citizens, such as Marian Anderson, Bill Cosby, Grace Kelly, Ed Bradley, and Dick Clark.

But there is another Philadelphia—one that cuts across the city's many neighborhoods and ethnic groups—that battles the same social problems other big cities face. These problems concern clergymen like the Reverend Jeffrey Leath, pastor of Mother Bethel A.M.E. Church, the oldest property in America continuously owned by African Americans. On a recent Sunday, he exhorted his parishioners to beware the "things you can't undo," to avoid the temptations that pervade the city. "Are you squirming yet?" he asks the men in dark suits and women in hats, and especially the young people. I sit in the balcony of this historic church,

once a station in the Underground Railroad, and think about faith: the faith it takes to try a new life in a strange land, the faith required to keep nourishing a dream even when the odds seem stacked against you.

In many ways, faith has propelled Pennsylvania forward. In the face of intolerance, William Penn created a new colony open to people of many beliefs. At Valley Forge and at Gettysburg, the soldiers' faith in their nation helped them overcome powerful obstacles. The people of Johnstown and Pittsburgh fashioned new cities out of scarred ones. In the early days, Pennsylvania was a land where everything was for the taking. By the twentieth century, conservationists and the state fostered a different ethic—one that sought to manage and preserve the state's rich resources. It helped renew our forests and clean our waterways.

Certainly Pennsylvania is not a utopia. The state still faces many challenges. But we are a resourceful people and hopefully will continue to nurture our beautiful backyard. When the problems facing my own city seem insurmountable, I think back to that Sunday at Mother Bethel Church when the Gospel Choir sang "I Go to the Rock." A woman soloist rose and stood by the piano. Before she began, all was quiet. But as her rich voice soared through chorus after chorus, feet tapped, hands clapped, and the choir's response resonated through the vaulted sanctuary. There was no escaping this music or the faith it conveyed.

All along my journey, I met Pennsylvanians who are fulfilling the promise of William Penn's Holy Experiment: the guides at Ephrata, Gettysburg, and Old Bedford Village who remind us of our historic past; the apple grower who helps make the state's farms so productive; the steelworkers who meet our industrial needs; and the Walter Costlows, Cork Wiricks, and Clancy Prevosts who leave their small Pennsylvania towns to make their way in the larger world, only to return and make their own contribution back home. I am glad to be home.

Fifty-four full-time gardeners
tend eleven thousand different
kinds of plants at Longwood
Gardens, one of America's fore-
most horticultural displays. ▶

George Washington's poorly equipped troops staggered into Valley Forge in December 1777 and built more than one thousand log huts to escape the cold. After six months of intensive training, the Continentals marched out of Valley Forge a disciplined fighting force. ◄ In the War for Independence, the British defeated American Revolutionary forces in the Battle of Brandywine, which is reenacted each September in Chadds Ford. ▲

Fox hunting is a family sport in Chester County. Riders are able to enjoy the rolling countryside while admiring how a tenacious pack of hounds pursues a fox, and how the wily fox outwits his pursuers. The hunt is over when the fox "goes to ground," slipping into a hole. ▲

Mr. Stewart's "Cheshire" foxhounds await the beginning of the hunt in Chester County. Since their eyesight is poor, English foxhounds must rely on their keen sense of smell to track the fox. ▲

Over one thousand acres of gardens, meadows, and woodlands attract eight hundred thousand visitors each year to Longwood Gardens, a former du Pont country estate in Kennett Square. ▲ Pennsylvania produces 370 million pounds of mushrooms annually. Pickers Eduardo Pantoja (foreground) and Angelo Burgos begin work as early as 3 A.M. ▶ Stephanie Magee feeds the thoroughbreds at a Chester County horse farm. ▶▶

In Gettysburg National Military Park, Union soldiers repulsed Pickett's charge, turning the tide of the Civil War. ◄ During his presidency, Dwight D. Eisenhower entertained world leaders such as de Gaulle and Khrushchev at his Gettysburg farm. After retiring, the general painted and practiced his golf swing within sight of the Civil War battlefield. ▲ A German communal society noted for its beautifully illuminated manuscripts and austere, disciplined lifestyle flourished at Ephrata Cloister in the 1700s. ►►

Maria English, a quality-assurance technician at Hershey Chocolate U.S.A., takes samples from a giant conch that grinds about ten thousand pounds of chocolate, making it smooth and creamy. ▲

Wanda Ruby paints a border on candy dishes at Pfaltzgraff, the oldest commercial pottery in America. The York-based company was founded by one of the state's many German potters during the early 1800s. Today, Pfaltzgraff combines old-world skills with modern technology. ▲

Ribbons of Asian pear trees blossom in the rolling hills of Adams County, home to twenty thousand acres of orchards. ▲ The fruit growers of Pennsylvania, the fifth-largest apple-producing state in the nation, harvest approximately 250 thousand tons of apples each autumn. ▶

Friends meetinghouses, like this one near Birdsboro, dot Pennsylvania's landscape and serve as a reminder of the tolerant, peace-loving Quaker principles that helped shape the commonwealth. ◄ The Walnut Street Bridge stretches across the broad Susquehanna River by Harrisburg, providing a vital link between the state capital and City Island. ▲ Over two hundred fifty thousand auto buffs converge on Hershey to view vintage cars at the Antique Automobile Club of America's eastern division fall meet. ►►

The Harley-Davidson plant in York is a mecca for motorcycle enthusiasts, who can watch workers assemble the latest models on the factory tour or inspect classic bikes at the adjoining museum. Gary Markle has "trued," or aligned, over two million wheels since 1973. ▲

Joe Humphreys hooks a trout in Yellow Breeches Creek near Boiling Springs. The Penn State professor and author has shared his angling secrets with thousands, including President Jimmy Carter. ▲ The rural ironmaking community of Hopewell Furnace supplied the American patriots with arms and ammunition during the American Revolution and, until 1883, manufactured items such as cookware, iron stoves, and pig iron. ►►

The Amish farmers of Lancaster County still use mule teams to pull their plows. They believe the Bible impels them to replenish the earth by tilling the soil by hand to produce an abundant harvest. ▲ Athough some Amish sects permit the use of dark-colored cars, the strictest sect, the Old Order Amish, rely on horse-drawn buggies. Models do not change from year to year, and with care, a carriage will last a couple throughout their lives. ▶

Once the site of iron furnaces—and later textile mills—Reading pioneered the concept of factory outlets in the 1960s. Over ten million shoppers converge on Reading each year, and the phenomenon of factory outlets has grown into a seven-billion-dollar industry nationwide. ◄ The 272-foot dome in Harrisburg's Capitol building was inspired by the dome of the Cathedral of St. Peter's in Rome. Four Edwin Austin Abbey murals decorate the inner dome, which towers above the rotunda's sweeping marble staircase. ▲

Though historians debate whether Betsy Ross sewed the first American flag in Philadelphia, workers such as Shirley Rabold still make Old Glory at Valley Forge Flag Company's Womelsdorf p ant. ▲ When flames razed Leonard Rohrbach's dairy barn in Shoemakersvil e, his neighbors—in true Pennsylvania Dutch style—helped him raise a new one. ▶

Over 130 species of wildflowers, such as these Virginia bluebells, blossom at Shenk's Ferry Wildflower Preserve, along the lower Susquehanna River. Indian remains in the area date back to A.D. 1400. ◄ Basket maker Marshall Seaman weaves a piece of Pennsylvania's history at Old Bedford Village, a reconstructed pioneer settlement in Bedford County. ▲

Two birches and an eastern redbud stand watch at a Westmoreland County forest preserve, where black bears forage for berries, wild turkeys chatter, and white-tailed deer curl up each night. ▲

Early morning fog rises over Raystown Lake, a magnet for boaters, swimmers, and fishermen in Huntingdon County. The thirty-mile lake was created between 1968 and 1978 by the U.S. Army Corps of Engineers as a flood-control measure in the Susquehanna River basin. ▲

Tractor pulls, grain threshing, corn shredding, and straw baling are all part of the Antique Tractor, Small Engine & Machinery Show at the Fulton County Fairgrounds in McConnellsburg. ▲ Coal trains now wind past St. Michael and across the meadow where Lake Conemaugh once stood. The lake, fourteen miles above Johnstown, "leaped out" when the South Fork Dam gave way, causing the tragic 1889 Johnstown Flood. ▶

A flower girl and ring bearer await the rest of the wedding party outside the First Lutheran Church in Johnstown. ◄ Completed in 1854, the Horseshoe Curve opened up rail travel between east and west by overcoming the steep grade of the Alleghenies—once thought virtually impassable by train—with an ingenious U-shaped bend above Altoona. ▲

During his lifetime, industrialist and philanthropist Andrew Carnegie amassed—and gave away—about 350 million dollars. The Carnegie, the cultural monument he bequeathed to Pittsburgh, contains the third-largest collection of dinosaur remains in the United States. ▲

White-water rafters and kayakers, such as Brendon Donnellan, tackle some of the East's most challenging rapids in the Youghiogheny River Gorge at Ohiopyle State Park. *Ohiopyle,* which boasts powerful falls, is derived from an Indian word meaning, "white frothy water." ▲

Fallingwater, a masterpiece of architect Frank Lloyd Wright's, was built overtop a waterfall in Mill Run. It served as the weekend home of Pittsburgh department-store magnate Edgar J. Kaufmann. ▲ Light filters through the stained glass windows at the Heinz Memorial Chapel, used for worship, concerts, and weddings at the University of Pittsburgh. ▶ Set where the Allegheny, Monongahela, and Ohio rivers join, Pittsburgh—one of the world's largest inland ports—was a fort in the French and Indian War. ▶▶

Wearing protective garb, ironworker Charles "Chuck" Yoest withstands the 2700° Fahrenheit heat emanating from the blast furnace at U.S. Steel's Edgar Thomson plant in Braddock. Built in 1875, the plant was Pittsburgh industrialist Andrew Carnegie's first steel mill. ◄ Following his motto, "To do a common thing uncommonly well," Henry John Heinz opened a pickle and relish factory in 1869. The Pittsburgh-based corporation now sells over three thousand products from 102 sites around the globe. ▲

The Narrows Overlook on Route 68 near East Brady offers a panoramic view of the Allegheny River—popular for its fishing, boating, and waterskiing—as it snakes its way south to Pittsburgh. ▲ McConnell's Mill State Park is named for the restored grist mill on Slippery Rock Creek, which ground corn, wheat, oats, and buckwheat until 1928. ▶

Like a ghost from the past, a costumed guide strolls through Old Economy Village in Ambridge, home to a nineteenth-century German communal society known for its winemaking and textiles. ◀ In spring, ostrich ferns uncurl their fronds in Raccoon Creek State Park. The park's wildflower reserve harbors more than five hundred species of flowering plants, including bull thistle, hepatica, jack-in-the-pulpit, wild ginger, and larkspur. ▲

A grape harvester at Archer and Pratz Vineyards picks the fragrant Concord grapes used in jams, jellies, juices, and wines. Pennsylvania's "Wine Country" stretches across thirteen thousand acres of Erie County and produces over eighty thousand tons of grapes each year. ▲

Visitors browse among more than one hundred fifty varieties of garden mums at the Paschke farm and stand near Lake Erie. For three generations, the Paschkes have been expanding their colorful selection of mums, which now carpet some fourteen acres in North East. ▲

After the flagship *Lawrence* was disabled, Commodore Oliver Hazard Perry transferred to the brig *Niagara,* where he hoisted his battle flag "Don't Give Up the Ship." The *Niagara,* now docked in Erie, went on to defeat the British in the War of 1812's Battle of Lake Erie. ▲ Presque Isle State Park's beaches jut seven miles into Lake Erie and attract over three hundred species of birds and about four million visitors each year. Presque Isle, a thirty-two-hundred-acre peninsula, is French for "almost an island." ▶

In 1859, Edwin Drake drilled the world's first commercial oil well, sparking an oil boom in northwestern Pennsylvania. The derrick has been carefully reconstructed on its original site in Titusville. ◀ Leonard Harrison and Colton Point state parks straddle Pennsylvania's "Grand Canyon," a forty-seven-mile gorge cut by glacial meltwater in the last Ice Age. ▲

After Joseph M. Fox was introduced to the game of golf on a trip to St. Andrews, Scotland, the wealthy Pennsylvanian brought the game back home. In 1887, he constructed the Foxburg Golf Course and Country Club, the oldest golf course in continuous use in the United States. ▲ Hearts Content Scenic Area protects American beech, hemlock, and white pine. ▶ Penn decreed religious freedom a cornerstone for his "Holy Experiment," and diverse houses of worship—including this East Point church—dot the state. ▶ ▶

90

Eastern elk once ranged throughout the commonwealth, but by 1867 the large herds had been decimated. The game commission introduced Rocky Mountain elk to the state in the early 1900s, and a herd still roams—protected from hunting—in Elk and Cameron counties. ◄ Pennsylvania's deciduous trees magically relive the Cinderella story each year, shedding their tired, green housedresses to become the belles of the ball. ▲

Unchecked lumbering almost destroyed the seemingly endless "Penn's Woods" during the 1800s. This leaf in the Allegheny National Forest evokes the comeback of the state's woodlands, which now flourish throughout a vast network of public parks and forests. ▲

Hundreds of families travel to Green Horizon Farm near Bloomsburg to cut down the "perfect" Christmas tree. Each year, more than 1.5 million evergreens are harvested throughout the state, especially in Indiana County, where a Queen Evergreen is crowned each spring. ▲

Penn State's diehard fans crowd Beaver Stadium's ninety-three thousand seats no matter how threatening the weather. One of the Nittany Lions' most storied rivalries is against the Pitt Panthers. ▲

Centre County's fertile valleys are home to many picturesque dairy farms. These holstein heifers at Valley Wide Farm are bred at sixteen months and become milk-producing cows after they turn two. ▲ Ivy crawls across the Philipsburg town hall, erected in 1887. The town was settled in 1797 by Philadelphians a few years after the Yellow Fever epidemic. A milestone for the old Philadelphia-to-Erie turnpike sits in front of the hall. ►►

Columbia County is home to rolling farmland and the Bloomsburg Fair, which attracts half a million fairgoers with its agricultural exhibits, marching bands, horse races, and top-name entertainers. ▲ Beavers built the first dam at Black Moshannon, and in the late 1800s a lumber company constructed a larger dam and saw mill at the same site. After the logging boom ended, the lake and surrounding bog became a state park. ▶ This barn near Benton has witnessed planting and harvesting for generations. ▶▶

Pennsylvania has nearly 1.2 million licensed hunters, and sportsmen pursue large and small game in its rich forests. In some rural counties, schoolchildren have off the first day of buck season. At the Penn State Deer Research Facility, students observe white-tailed deer up close. ◄ During the eighteenth century, Philadelphians produced some of the finest furniture made in Colonial America. In Lewisburg, Pennsylvania House cabinet-makers, such as Henry Aurand, continue the tradition of crafting fine furniture. ▲

Thirteen-mile Lake Wallenpaupack was created in 1926 when Wallenpaupack Creek was dammed to provide hydroelectric power. The popular Pocono Mountains vacation destination derives its name from the Indian word meaning "the stream of swift and slow water." ▲

The everyday life of the coal miner is preserved at Eckley Miners' Village, a company "patch" town in the anthracite country found in northeastern Pennsylvania. Since 1971, it has been listed as a national register district and is now home to retired miners and their families. ▲

After falling on hard times, the towns of Mauch Chunk and East Mauch Chunk merged in 1954, and the new borough took the name of Jim Thorpe, the great Native American Olympian, who is buried there. The Victorian town has become a popular tourist destination. ▲

Engineer Robert Patterson reminisces about the glory days of railroading at Steamtown National Historic Site in Scranton. Visitors can tour the railyard and roundhouse of the old Delaware, Lackawanna & Western line or ride an antique steam train into the Poconos. ▲

More than one million skiers take to the slopes in the Pocono Mountains each winter. With eighty-six illuminated trails, night skiing has become popular at many resorts, including Big Boulder. ▲

Deer Leap, Factory, and Fulmer Falls
(pictured) tumble down Dingmans Creek in Child's Park, part of the Delaware
Water Gap National Recreation Area. For twenty-five miles, the Appalachian Trail
cuts through the park, and hikers may spy bald eagle, black bear, and bobcat. ▲

With about two hundred twenty covered bridges, Pennsylvania has more "kissing bridges" than any other state. The Forksville Bridge crosses Loyalsock Creek with a single span of 156 feet. ▲ A striped maple and a yellow birch breathe in the spray of ninety-four-foot Ganoga Falls, tallest of twenty-two named waterfalls in Ricketts Glen State Park. ▶ Early travelers thought they had reached the end of the world as they journeyed through the wild, S-shaped valley that is now home to Worlds End State Park. ▶ ▶

At D. G. Yuengling & Son in Pottsville, Dick Yuengling Jr. (left) and brewmaster Ray Norbert overlook the brew kettle. Yuengling's great great-grandfather began America's oldest brewery in 1829. ◄ Cyclists from around the world race through the mountainous Pocono stage of the Tour du Pont, before heading south on their one-thousand-mile course. ▲ Fog shrouds Flagstaff Mountain, above Jim Thorpe. The town was once home to Asa Packer, who founded the Lehigh Valley Railroad and Lehigh University. ►►

The Delaware River twists through the Kittatinny Ridge to create the Delaware Water Gap. This sinuous gap cuts between New Jersey's Mount Tammany (left) and Pennsylvania's Mount Minsi. ▲ Glacial winters and summer thaws gradually wrested the boulders in Hickory Run State Park from two nearby ridges more than twenty thousand years ago. ▶ The First Bank of the United States served as the government's bank from 1797 to 1811. The neo-classic building sits in Independence National Historical Park. ▶▶

Caught in a disagreement with the violin-makers guild in his native Germany, C. F. Martin, Sr., moved his guitar-making business to America in 1833. Craftsmen such as Tim Teel, who is hand-fitting the neck to the body, still make prized Martin guitars in Nazareth. ◀ By mixing paraffin wax and powdered pigments, Binney & Smith produces over two billion Crayola crayons each year. At their Easton headquarters, material handler Lauren Kahler inspects crayons for shipment to over sixty countries. ▲

Using precise strokes, a member of the Philadelphia Girls Rowing Club skims across the Schuylkill River in her sculling shell. During much of the year, the Schuylkill Navy supervises rowing regattas. ▲ In a whirl of string bands, feathered floats and flamboyant costumes, twenty thousand mummers strut down Philadelphia's Broad Street on New Year's Day. ▶

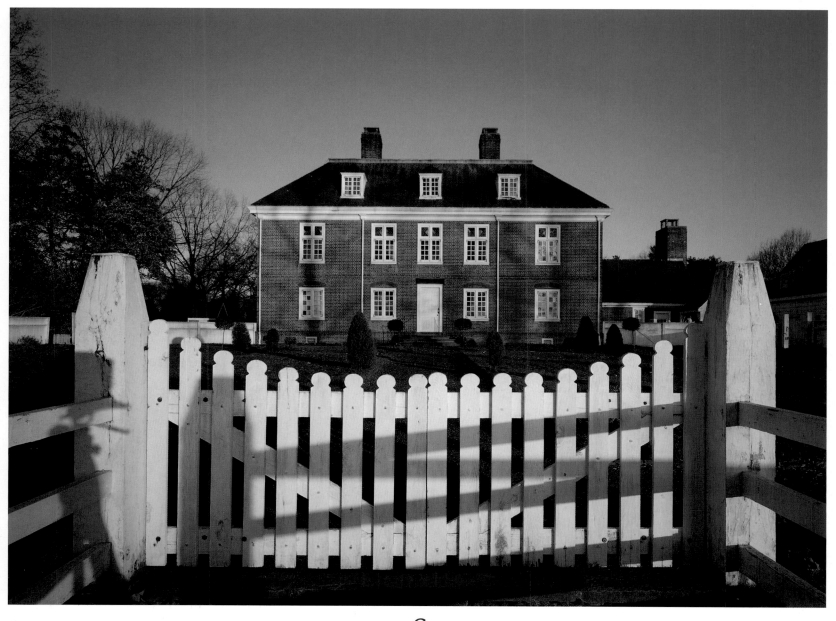

Sunburst-shaped holes ventilate the hay drying inside this Bucks County barn, constructed in Riegelsville about 1784. ◄ William Penn's country estate, Pennsbury Manor, has been rebuilt on its original foundation. Although Penn resided here only two years, the Georgian manor house, formal gardens, orchard, and vineyard reflect his wealth and status. ▲ For decades, no buildings in Philadelphia rose higher than William Penn's statue atop 548-foot City Hall. But in the 1980s, a new skyline of skyscrapers rose. ►►

Jacques Lipchitz sculpture provides a modern counterpoint to the classical edifice of the Philadelphia Museum of Art. The museum's extensive collections include works by Pennsylvania artists Mary Cassatt, Andrew Wyeth, Andy Warhol, Alexander Calder, and Thomas Eakins. ▲ Big Bird, Ernie, and Cookie Monster greet visitors to Sesame Place in Langhorne. ▶ New varieties of salvia, marigolds, and petunias flourish in the experimental gardens at Fordhook Farm, the Doylestown estate of the Burpee family. ▶▶

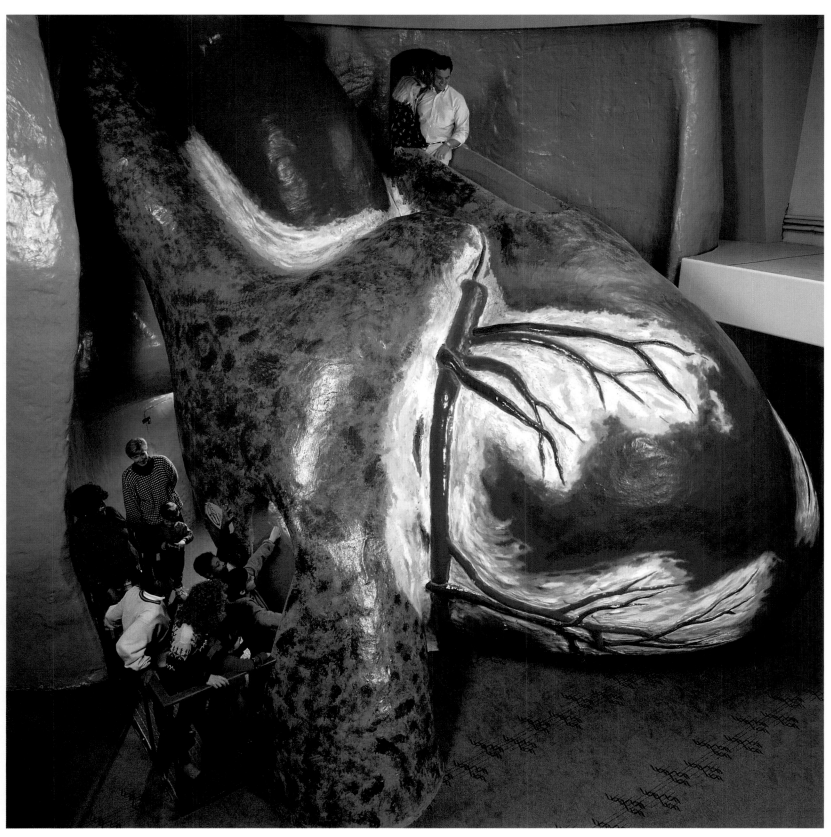

Parishioners gather at Mother Bethel A.M.E. Church, the oldest property in the nation continuously owned by African Americans. Founded in 1787, it was once an Underground Railroad station. ◄ Visitors tour the heart, one of the most popular exhibits at the Franklin Institute Science Museum. The Philadelphia museum is a fitting monument to Benjamin Franklin, whose heart still beats beneath the metropolis he helped shape. ▲

Ascant fifteen feet of brick and cobblestone divides the homes along Elfreth's Alley in Philadelphia. Dating from 1702, it is known as the oldest continuously occupied residential street in America. ▲

In 1740, Benjamin Franklin helped found Philadelphia Academy, now the University of Pennsylvania. The school began the nation's first medical school (1765) and the first collegiate business school (1881). In 1946, the world's first computer, *ENIAC,* was unveiled here. ▲

Cast in 1752 to celebrate the fiftieth anniversary of William Penn's Charter of Privileges, the Liberty Bell symbolizes American freedom. Visitors touch the cracked bell and read its biblical inscription: "Proclaim liberty throughout all the land, unto all the inhabitants thereof." ▲ Nearly everyone who visits the Betsy Ross House in Philadelphia, including this Girl Scout troop, poses in front of the eighteenth-century flag maker's home. ▶

Acknowledgments
by H. Mark Weidman

THOUGH I HAVE LIVED in Pennsylvania most of my forty years, I did not really get to know my home state until I photographed for this book. Ironically, it took a trip to Siberia to land the assignment. Doug Pfeiffer of Graphic Arts Center Publishing had been on my mailing list for several years when I sent him a promotional piece about my upcoming photo trip to Siberia. On the response postcard, he simply wrote: "Any interest in doing a whole photo book on Pennsylvania?" The rest, as they say, is history. My first thank you goes to Graphic Arts Center Publishing for giving me the opportunity to photograph PENNSYLVANIA.

Deciding what to include in a book of this scope can prove challenging. My wife, writer Marjorie Ackermann, spoke with people at many state agencies and all of the tourist promotion agencies around the state. They sent us reams of literature and talked—often in great detail—about their corner of the state. We thank them for the leads!

Over the course of three years, it took many trips and fifty thousand miles to complete the photography in PENNSYLVANIA. A grant from the Pennsylvania Council on the Arts helped with my expenses as did Polaroid Corporation's generous contribution of film. Along the way, I met many wonderful people, some of whom appear in this book. Shawnees Dan Moluntha Wright and Ken Shooting Star were especially accommodating, traveling to High Knob Overlook and standing patiently while I photographed them during a bitter cold sunset. And I will never forget the folks at Carnegie Mellon's Robotics Institute, who brought "Virgil" out for an evening stroll in Schenley Park.

Many others helped behind the scenes, including the mechanics at North Penn Imports, who kept breathing life into my aging VW van; and Dave Pry, who enabled me to explore the mysterious bog at Black Moshannon by lending me a rental canoe at 5 A.M.! The Bitlers took time from their busy farming schedule to help me photograph a cow with her calf—no easy task. Since I am not an equestrian, I relied on Mrs. John B. Hannum and her battered Jeep Wagoneer to follow a fox hunt. She taught me the difference between a dog and a hound.

When not camping, I stayed in many lodgings across Pennsylvania, but none more hospitable than the Flora Villa Inne in Eagles Mere, where Jay and Shannon welcomed Marjorie and me several times. I also appreciate the assistance of the folks at Allenberry Inn on the Yellow Breeches Creek, where I photographed fly fisherman Joe Humphreys.

I am indebted to the many companies, historic sites, institutions, and farms around the state that allowed me to photograph on their premises; and to the Pennsylvania Historical and Museum Commission, which granted permission to photograph some of their sites.

Marjorie and I would also like to thank the many Pennsylvanians who agreed to be interviewed and later took the time to help her "fact check" the text. The suggestions of Elizabeth Costa and Michael Schwager, who read the first draft, also proved invaluable.

Many freelance assistants helped with the photography, especially Lisa Kern, Kelly Dillon, Michael O'Neill, Ken Williams, Bill Hrovoski, and Alex Jones; and Jim Airgood of Terry Wilde Studios. Carolyn Kemp deserves a medal for cheerfully labeling thousands of Pennsylvania transparencies. And I appreciate the care Bud Mills and his staff at Professional Color in Philadelphia gave to processing my film.

Marjorie and I also wish to thank our friends and families for their support. We appreciate the warm hospitality of the Kraemer family, who helped us with several photos. And we are grateful to our neighbors, Ed and Jean Goodwin, who generously lent us a generator and later provided a boat to photograph Lake Wallenpaupack; and Dick and Loretta Reeder, who watched Christopher and Chelsea during the last-minute crunches a project of this size demands. Finally, we thank Isabelle and Guenter Ackermann, who in many ways helped this labor of love become a reality.